AN

A STORY OF LOVE

SOMEWHERE IN THE EVENING SKY A LITTLE ANGEL LIVED ON A PUFFY WHITE CLOUD. HER NAME WAS ANGELINE.

ONE DAY SHE SAW HERSELF IN A SHINY RAINDROP....

....AND REALIZED THAT HER
WINGS WERE VERY, VERY
SMALL.

ANGELINE TRIED TO THINK
OF WAYS TO MAKE THEM
LOOK BIGGER.

"I KNOW, I'LL GLUE EXTRA
CURLY FUZZY FEATHERS ALL
OVER THEM". . . .

. . .BUT THEY JUST BLEW OFF.

THEN SHE THOUGHT, "I'LL
PAINT THEM BRIGHT COLORS",
AND RAN FOR A BRUSH. . .

. . BUT SHE JUST LOOKED
FUNNY.

SHE EVEN TRIED TO
HIDE THEM UNDER A
GIANT, ENORMOUS STRAW
HAT WITH LOTS AND LOTS
OF FANCY FLOWERS...

...BUT SHE JUST LOOKED
SILLY.

ANGELINE FELT VERY
SAD. "HOW COULD ANYONE
LOVE AN ANGEL WITH
SUCH ITSY-BITSY WINGS?"
SHE SOFTLY WHISPERED.

THEN SHE STARTED
TO CRY.

AS SHE GENTLY WIPED AWAY A TEAR, SHE FELT A BUMP. A BIG, DARK CLOUD BLEW BY AND ALMOST KNOCKED HER OVER. ANGELINE WATCHED IT SLIDE PAST AND SADLY THOUGHT, "I'LL ALWAYS LOOK STRANGE. I CAN'T FIX MY WINGS AND THEY WILL NEVER GROW."

SUDDENLY SHE HAD AN IDEA.

"I'LL JUMP INTO THIS CLOUD AND SAIL FAR AWAY INTO THE SKY WHERE NO ONE WILL EVER SEE ME." SO SHE HOPPED ON THE FLUFFY CLOUD AND FLOATED LIKE A BIG, WHITE BUBBLE INTO THE STILL BLUE NIGHT.

WITH A BIG SIGH, THE LITTLE ANGEL TUCKED HERSELF IN AND FELL FAST ASLEEP. BUT AS SHE GLIDED ALONG SHE BEGAN TO SLOWLY SINK DEEPER AND DEEPER INTO THE CLOUD'S SOFT, BLACK CENTER.

ANGELINE TUMBLED UPSIDEDOWN AND SIDEWAYS UNTIL....

SHE FINALLY LANDED ON
THE BOTTOM WITH A
GENTLE THUD.

SHE WAS ALL ALONE AND
VERY, VERY SCARED.

SUDDENLY SHE LOOKED DOWN
AND SAW A BEAUTIFUL
RAINBOW.

"OH MY," SHE SIGHED, "MAYBE
IF I JUMP ON THIS
RAINBOW IT WILL TAKE
ME SOMEWHERE....
  ANYWHERE....   AWAY
FROM THIS GLOOMY, SAD
  PLACE."
ANGELINE BEGAN TO SLIDE
  DOWN...DOWN... DOWN

        UNTIL...

            THUMP!

SHE LANDED ON A SOFT
WARM BLANKET.
ANGELINE COULD SEE
NOTHING IN THE SHADOWS.
"OH NO, ANOTHER SCARY
PLACE."
THE ANGEL STARED INTO
THE DARKNESS AND
REALIZED SHE WAS ON
A LITTLE GIRL'S BED.

THEN SHE SAW THE
LITTLE GIRL . ...HIDING
BEHIND A BIG PILLOW.

"I'M SO AFRAID OF THE DARK,"
SHE WHISPERED.

"I KNOW JUST HOW YOU FEEL," ANGELINE CRIED. "BUT I'M HERE NOW SO YOU DON'T HAVE TO BE FRIGHTENED ANYMORE." AND WITH THAT THE LITTLE GIRL SCOOPED UP THE ANGEL IN HER ARMS AND HELD HER TIGHT.

HER TEARS DRIED, HER
CRIES STOPPED AND
SHE DRIFTED OFF TO
SLEEP

ANGELINE NEVER FELT SO
LOVED AND CARED FOR.
SHE WAS SO HAPPY THAT
EVEN HER WINGS LOOKED
A LITTLE BIGGER.
AND FROM THAT DAY ON
THE LITTLE GIRL AND
THE ANGEL WERE TOGETHER,
EACH HELPING THE OTHER
IN THEIR OWN WAY.

AND JUST AS THERE ARE
STARS IN THE SKY, THERE'S
A SPECIAL ANGEL FOR
EVERY LITTLE GIRL AND
BOY....... WAITING TO
BE HELD AND LOVED.